A Scent of Frangipani

Also by Jill Nevile and published by Ginninderra Press
A Scent of Pines

Jill Nevile

A Scent of Frangipani

Acknowledgements

Many of the poems in this collection – sometimes in a different form – have previously been published in the following newspapers and literary magazines: *Peninsula News, The Mozzie,* and *Multi Arts Confederation News Sheet.*

Poems have also appeared in the following anthologies: *The Poetry Project* 2006 & 2007 (WEA Sydney), *Wild* and *First Refuge* (Ginninderra Press), *Seeking the Sun* (Central Coast Poets Inc.), *Great Green Limericks, Coastal – A Pack of Poems about Places.*

Thanks to Maddie, Georgy and Bertie
for all the love and laughter

A Scent of Frangipani
ISBN 978 1 76109 105 6
Copyright © text Jill Nevile 2021
Front cover photo: Jill Nevile
Back cover photo: Jill with pet dog Bertie, by Liz Kennedy

First published 2021 by
GINNINDERRA PRESS
PO Box 3461 Port Adelaide 5015
www.ginninderrapress.com.au

Contents

Home and Abroad

Scent of Frangipani	9
Winter at Ettalong	10
Garden Bells	11
Among the Mangroves	12
Plover Power	13
Eucalypt	14
Outback Wave	15
View From the Quay	16
Sydney Storm	17
Gods That Thunder	18
Sounds of the Isles	19
Island Impressions	20
Xairete, Amorgos	21
Maniots	22
Athene's Gift	23
The Voice	24
Under Ground	25
Theo's Story	26
Supermoon	28
Remember Us	29
On Deck	30

Personal Poems

Here's to You, Miss Edwards	33
Days of Wine and Lotus	34
The Necklace	35
Garden of Memory	36
Life Without Maddie	37
At Play on Mount Olympus	38

Biding My Time	39
Behind the Hibiscus	40
Prickly	41
Misogynist Myth	42
The Day the Kookaburra Called	43
Acerbic Zone	44
Immobile	45
The Musician	46
Let Me Go	47
Fields of Gold	48
Dear Francesca	49
Finding My New Home	50
A Basket of Apricots	51
Surfeit	53
Thief	54
The Dream in My Pocket	55
Just Dreaming	56

The Lighter Side

Poetic Potions	59
Gleaming	60
The Teddy Bear's Downfall	61
A Girl's Best Friend	62
Paradise Found	63
My Fate	64
Limericks	65
Oven Gloves	66
Trollittering	67
Metromania	68

Home and Abroad

Scent of Frangipani

I need a break, I often say,
Then go outside to spend the day
In the place of my delight –
The garden – such a welcome sight
And there I stay.

It is so easy to delay
Things that should be done today,
Those letters, poems I should write –
I need a break.

Roses blossoming in May,
Fragrant frangipani spray,
Velvet petals, creamy white
Keep me there until the night.
Can I tear myself away?
I need a break.

Winter at Ettalong

After the storm –
Clouds fragment in a sky
The colour of cornflowers.
Sunlight skims the water,
Breezes dry the atmosphere
And ring bells on the boats
That have sheltered in the bay.
Where tides rippled the sand
Seagulls dip for morsels.
People and pets come out of hiding
To gaze on an indigo sea
And plants, rinsed by the rain,
Spread their leaves and breathe
In the freshly-laundered air.

Garden Bells

I love your dainty, hanging bells
That bloom in such profusion
All along those stately stems,
Extravagant effusion.

In lavender or fuchsia-pink,
Your bells attract the bee,
Speckled markings show the way
To set the pollen free.

Your leaves make digitalis,
Healing it imparts,
Such luscious purple clusters,
Foxglove – a plant for hearts.

Among the Mangroves

Away from the rolling ocean,
The bracing scent of the sea,
I miss the sound
Of the ceaseless waves.
The rhythmic constancy.

A breeze caressed my cheekbones,
Tousled through my hair,
I could almost taste
The salty tang
That lingered in the air.

Yet I have found contentment
At another waterside,
Where the sea laps,
Stroking the sand,
By an ocean pacified.

Bobbing boats are tethered,
Watchful pelicans preen,
A multitude
Of mangrove trees
Frame this restful scene.

Plover Power

I chose a Woy Woy garden,
There to make a scrape.
I guarded and protected it
And hoped to find a mate.

A female plover took a look,
Her yellow mask was fine,
I courted her and mated,
Those speckled eggs were mine.

I stayed nearby as lookout,
As she sat on the nest,
Whenever there was danger,
I answered her request.

To some it may seem risky,
Eggs laid on the ground,
But we have special armoury,
For which we are renowned.

We can flare our dark grey wings
To make a threatening cloak,
Those wings have spurs like daggers,
Shrieks sound a warning note.

I'm a spur-winged plover,
Let my name be heard,
Also called masked lapwing,
A cloak and dagger bird.

Eucalypt

Gum tree
that graces my garden
your irregular outline pleases me
with branches like arms that stretch over fences
so kookaburras, currawongs and butcherbirds
can perch – to call and chatter in the foliage
cockatoos also screech on those branches
and tear twigs from your arms
to toss on my flowerbeds
and you, too, are untidy
when you disrobe
casting rolls of
burnt parchment
far and wide
but after rain
when a creamy
trunk glistens
in the moonlight
all is forgiven
as you soar in a gown of glaze

Outback Wave

At the end of a dusty path,
Almost hidden behind the trees,
A wall of rock soars
In a steep curve,
A fifteen-metre overhang
Of massive cresting wave.

Myriad years of wind
And rain have sculpted
This granite outcrop,
Minerals painting the stone
With sweeping bands of
Red, silver, orange and gold.

I climb to the top,
Imagine riding the surf
So far from the ocean.
But the rock draws me
Back to its base,
Overwhelmed
By the outback tsunami.

View From the Quay

When I go down to Sydney town I head for Circular Quay,
To watch the jaunty ferries bustling through the sea.
The Opera House, it seems to float, it shimmers in the sun,
Symbol of the city, its reputation won.

While strolling round I like to read what other writers said,
Their comments fixed in pavement plaques beneath the walker's tread,
I share with C.J. Dennis his pleasure and surprise.
'The Bridge,' he said. 'I never dreamed! That arch that cut the skies!'

The cool Botanic Gardens, retreat from busy street,
For solo contemplation, or place for friends to meet,
Where bats called flying foxes hang from branches in the sky,
And many birds are bold enough to share my food supply.

I walk around the headland to Mrs Macquarie's Chair
To wonder at the beauties of Sydney Harbour fair,
Bewitched by its attractions, for this delight alone,
I feel so very lucky that this city's now my home.

Sydney Storm

In the Opera House, Prospero conjured a tempest.
As he raised his staff, lights flashed,
Sound thundered through the theatre,
Gales blew curtains into towering waves.

Outside, wind had whipped up the sea,
Thunder resounded round the harbour,
Lightning cracked the shell of night,
Pads of snow, hard as coins, pelted
Pavements amid the drenching rain.

Streets resembled rivers,
Streams flowed through parks,
Steps became waterfalls.

Such Shakespearean sorcery.

Gods That Thunder

On the outskirts of a town
In north-east Greece
Lies a tumbledown temple,
With surviving floors
Of marvellous mosaics.

Dominating town and temple
Is Mount Olympus,
Its secret summit veiled.
No wonder ancients quaked
When Zeus loosed his thunderbolts
And cracked the sky.

They needed their temple
To pacify
Those temperamental gods.

Sounds of the Isles

Now in my ears I hear the Sirens' call,
They sing a song that generates a yen,
Their dulcet tones are destined to enthral
And lure me back to Hellas once again.

The tap of donkey hooves on cobbled street –
So much more restful than the traffic noise –
Those tinkling bells of goats that sound so sweet
And crowing roosters crown my rural joys.

A swish of dolphin escorts as I sail
Between the islands in a jewelled sea,
They ride the waves leaving a creamy trail,
As ships slice through the ocean quay to quay.

Bouzouki music welcomes me ashore,
So I can hear those island sounds once more.

Island Impressions

I remember
A snowy monastery clinging to a cliff,
Seeming to melt into the mountain.
Winding streets where cafés perch on steps
And tavernas overlook a horseshoe harbour.

I remember
Waking to the crow of the rooster,
Opening shutters to soft sunshine
And cool air scented with jasmine.
Breakfasting on my balcony
To the sound of goat bells on the hillside
And a view of the still-sleepy port.

I remember
Wanting to stay longer
In this Aegean Arcadia.

Andio, Amorgos – till next year.

* *Andio* is Greek for goodbye.

Xairete, Amorgos

Drawn by sweet memories,
I returned to Amorgos.

To breakfast on a cool balcony,
Soothed by the tinkling bells
Of goats grazing on the hillside.

To walk the tracks linking villages,
Fields and unfrequented beaches.

To sit beside tranquil water
With a book, sipping a drink
And later, as I dined,
To see the harbour lights
Reflected in a glassy sea.

To meet again a companion
From last year – an unexpected
Harmony of travel plans.

And on warm, still evenings,
To watch a blood-orange sun
Slide into the blue Aegean.

* *Xairete* is a Greek greeting.

Maniots

Far from Greece's mainland, in the southern Peloponnese,
The Mani – a rugged region of rocky mountains –
Stretches a tentacle into the Mediterranean.

Harsh landscape breeds tough characters,
Rebellious, self-sufficient, often insular,
Villagers may have never left their birthplace
And know little of Greece beyond their home.
Isolated on their wild peninsula,
Maniots have a distinctive dialect,
As if to stress their separateness.

Many live a simple life,
Harvesting olives, tending goats,
Coaxing crops from stony soil.
At times of feuds and vendettas,
Maniots built homes like fortresses –
Stark stone towers high on the hills,
Strongholds for protection
And to watch for alien invaders.

Yet travellers need not fear
These independent inhabitants.
There is always a welcome
For discerning travellers
Who value the traditional ways
Of this unfrequented outpost.

Athene's Gift

What a wonder is the olive tree,
A worthy plant to grow and cultivate,
The fruit and oil are balm to you and me.

Its drought-resistant toughness is the key
That causes it to thrive and germinate,
What a wonder is the olive tree.

An olive branch is there for all to see,
To indicate that conflict can abate.
The fruit and oil are balm to you and me.

Symbolic oil is offered with a plea,
In herbal healing, leaves alleviate,
What a wonder is the olive tree.

Those ancient gods together did agree
An olive is the tree to venerate,
The fruit and oil are balm to you and me.

Athene's offering evolved to be
A precious plant that we can celebrate.
What a wonder is the olive tree,
The fruit and oil are balm to you and me.

The Voice

In a voice like a stream
From the mountains of Greece,
She sings her lyrics
With clarity of diction
And elegance.

A song can be a rivulet,
Performed with delicacy,
Or cascades of music
Breaking like surf
Over the audience.

Her modulations –
Ripples in a lament,
Waves in a refrain –
Ebb and flow with feeling
And passion.

From arias to taverna tunes,
Songs pour out of her
In many languages,
Like water flowing
From a natural spring.

Under Ground

Beneath the streets of London
Lies an enormous loom.
Speeding shuttles weave side to side,
Up and down, under and over,
Criss-crossing at different levels
To make an intricate pattern.

But, like Penelope's weaving,
The work is never finished,
For in the night hours,
When the loom is still,
Shuttles slide into sidings
And the strands disintegrate.

Theo's Story

I always was a working dog,
Never been a pet,
My training made me tough and strong
And disinclined to fret.

My job was in the army,
I used my trusty nose
To hunt for high explosives,
So vital to expose.

I lived in army kennels,
I was no pampered pooch,
But even hardy spaniels
Are partial to a smooch.

My master's name was Liam,
We worked together well,
He with modern weapons,
I with sense of smell.

One day when we were searching,
I heard a fearful sound,
My master fell and lay quite still
On that hostile ground.

I licked his face and whimpered,
But he did not respond.
They took me back to kennels,
Despite our special bond.

They treated me with kindness,
But I felt destitute.
That night I had a seizure,
Fatal for this recruit.

We went back home together,
My ashes with his tomb.
They honoured us as comrades
On that day of gloom.

Army dog-handler Liam Tasker was shot and killed in Afghanistan in March 2012. Theo died just hours later. They were repatriated to Britain together.

Supermoon

14 November 2016

Your people trampled my surface
And planted a flag in my space,
Tonight I came near
Simply to peer
At the earthlings' planetary base.

Remember Us

We are the animals you had to leave behind,
Donkeys that carried your goods,
Horses that pulled your ploughs,
Cows, sheep and goats that gave you milk and wool,
Until the bombs fell.

Wild creatures know how to survive,
But we relied on you for food and care.
Desperate, you fled with family and what little you could take.
Kind people give us what they can,
Yet many of us die.

Dogs and cats that roam the streets rummaging for scraps,
We were your pets, your guards, your mousers,
Birds that kept you company perished in cages.
We too are victims of war, with nowhere to go.
Remember us.

On Deck

Morning
A view through the porthole
Of steely blue water.

Midday
Sun transforms the sea
To the colour of cornflowers.

Afternoon
Silver tints the swell
Of the creamy surf.

Evening
Our ship slices through waves
Of liquid pewter.

Night
The sky, cloaked in sable,
Turns ocean to ink.

Personal Poems

Here's to You, Miss Edwards

When I was young and immature,
At the end of my first love affair,
In despair, I talked of suicide.
Miss Edwards listened,
All she said was –
No man is worth that.

Throughout my life,
When left bereft by love,
I've remembered her words.
My personal oracle
Telling me –
No one is worth that.

Her maxim served me well
In professional work.
Rejection, mortification,
Depression after reprimand,
I knew she would say,
No job is worth that.

When overwhelmed by grief,
Or utter humiliation,
Smouldering under injustice,
Resenting unfairness,
I've never forgotten –
Nothing is worth that.

Days of Wine and Lotus

Have you been to Lotus-land
To taste the sweet ambrosia?
Those who journeyed back from Troy
Discovered it near Kythira.

They ate the luscious golden fruit
That grows upon the lotus trees,
Lost all desire to travel home,
Ignored their leader's earnest pleas.

The lotus fruit is like a balm,
Its soothing power sedates the brain,
With its enchantment sounds recede
And memories begin to wane.

Lotophagi lived at ease
In afternoons of indolence,
Their daily dose of opiate
Ensured enduring somnolence.

Such languor I experienced
Lounging by a swimming pool,
Where robed attendants pampered me
And waving fan palms kept me cool.

Euphoric days of idleness,
Seductive though they seemed to be,
Wove restless, unproductive dreams
And stifled creativity.

The Necklace

I wore it on New Year's Eve,
My birth sign on a gold chain,
But as I unclasped it, I saw
A section of chain had tarnished.

I remembered a Christmas
More than fifty years ago,
When a lover linked it
Around my neck, with a kiss.

Eventually, as sometimes happens,
Our affair acquired tarnish,
Though not, till now, reflected in the chain
Or my pleasure in wearing the necklace.

Garden of Memory

I knew I had to leave you
Lying in the loam,
Your silken hair a simple shroud,
The garden soil your home.
I laid you in that earthen tomb,
A day of unremitting gloom.

I never marked your place of rest,
But made an indoor shrine –
A poem and your picture,
Beloved dog of mine,
I never need to tie a knot
To recollect that chosen spot.

I know that after all the years
Your body's fed the ground
Beneath your special snuffling site
Where birds and flowers abound,
Although your grave is left behind,
You will never leave my mind.

Life Without Maddie

I miss you at daybreak,
My gentle morning call,
Your furry face my first sight –
Now I see a vacant wall.

I miss you in the morning,
So full of life you'd gambol
Along the pathways of our walks –
Now I take a lonely stroll.

I miss you in the afternoon,
Dozing in satisfaction,
Persuading me to take a break –
Now I work without distraction.

I miss you coming home,
Your warm presence lying in wait,
Making joyful cries to greet me –
Now I reach a lifeless gate.

I miss you in the evening,
Time together on our own,
You curled up around my feet –
Now I have an empty home.

I miss you at nightfall,
Your eager footstep on the stair,
To settle down beside my bed –
Now I know you are not there.

At Play on Mount Olympus

Do you remember that hot Greek night
When we dined on wine and watermelon?
Sipped the sweet nectar,
Kissed wine from warm lips,
Then plunged our teeth into
Ambrosia of soft pink flesh.

Ah! that night we were gods.

Biding My Time

Dormant for decades,
I lie supine near the spine
Of the body that let me in
When it was very young.

If stress disturbs me,
I may attack the nerves,
But the body in its seventies,
Especially female, is my taste.

I erupt without warning,
Disturbing even the
Soundest sleeper with
Searing pain.

I target vulnerable spots,
Where I can do the most damage.
Treatment may suppress me,
But the pangs continue.
Nerves take months to heal.

Watch for the rash.
I am inside,
Waiting.

Behind the Hibiscus

I sit at my desk
With the ticking clock,
Indoors, nothing stirs.
Then, a sudden sound –
A dog shaking his ears.

I work in the garden
With the songs of the birds,
Outdoor harmony,
Then, a sudden tinkle –
A dog's disc as he walks.

I lie in my bed
With the beat of my heart,
Drifting, peacefully.
Then, a sudden patter –
A dog's feet on the floor.

It's a mean trick
Played by memories.
For my dog lies
Behind the hibiscus –
Under the soil.

Prickly

What can we do about challenging people
Who think they are always right?
They are quick to anger and take offence
At comments perceived as a slight.

You have to take care with your actions and words,
As they bristle at random remarks.
They point out your faults, but if you mention theirs,
You feel threatened by predatory sharks.

These people are full of what they want to say,
But omit to ask about you.
Their emphatic opinions accept no dissent,
For them, there is no other view.

Difficult types want things as they like,
They're in love with their own control.
They can seem to be friendly, but suddenly turn
And take an irascible role.

They expect us to welcome a ring at the bell
Whenever they choose to arrive,
Never thinking it might be a bad time to call –
How can such relationships thrive?

Misogynist Myth

It is written –

Of the ten parts of desire
Women possess nine,
So dangerous – they must be
Covered and controlled,
Lest they tempt weak men
With a glance or lock of hair.

Aren't men said to be
The stronger sex?

These men – who have only
One part of desire –
Why do they touch,
Proposition, abuse and rape,
Then blame women for their
Lack of self-control?

Avoid inflaming female passions,
Let men hide their bodies
From the lustful gaze of women.

The Day the Kookaburra Called

The day new neighbours arrived
A kookaburra came to call.
It perched on the fence,
Regarded me with interest
And posed for photographs.

A model visitor –
This cool kookaburra
Soothed me with its
Unruffled stillness.
No cackling or raucous laughter,
An omen – perhaps –
Of quiet neighbours.

Acerbic Zone

They were fermenting,
Those bitter feelings,
Seething beneath the surface
Of comforting friendship.

We shared secrets,
Dined together, telephoned,
Yet, unknown to me,
The subsoil bubbled.

The blast left me breathless,
Words scalding my ears,
Tone like rancorous lava
Scorching a rift between us.

Dazed by the onslaught,
I stand on the cracked crust,
As your diatribe echoes
Around the caustic caldera.

Immobile

A working day
On a city street,
A black dog
Lies on the road,
Immobile, among cars
Stopped at the lights.

A scooter rider dismounts,
Gently moves the body
To the central mound,
She can do no more.
I can do nothing
Amid furious traffic.

Then, from nearby,
Comes a sound
I cannot forget,
From the core of his being,
An animal howl
Of a man in torment.

The Musician

With that body he knows she will be resonant.
He caresses the curves,
Fingers the indentations,
Plucks at the strings,
Varying the tension,
Patiently tuning her up.

Feeling the vibrations,
A zing in the strings,
He plays her with passion
And rhythmic movements.
She reverberates
With sweet sounds
That rise and rise
Till the symphony reaches crescendo.

Let Me Go

with acknowledgement to Dylan Thomas

Let me go gently into that good night,
If quality of life is all but dead,
When the future is no longer bright.

For life at any cost I will not fight,
Dependent helplessness is what I dread.
Let me go gently into that good night.

This is the will and testament I write
For those that care for me, to cut the thread,
When the future is no longer bright.

A pet in pain would be a case to cite,
It should not suffer, why must I instead?
Let me go gently into that good night.

I am convinced a person has the right
To choose the peaceful path of death to tread,
When the future is no longer bright.

Heed my words; have pity on my plight,
Do not prolong the final days abed.
Let me go gently into that good night,
When the future is no longer bright.

Fields of Gold

How I remember, how I remember,
We walked in fields of gold,
You – my perfect companion
Rewarded love tenfold.
You left me many years ago,
When you grew frail and old.
The joys we found together
Could not have been foretold.
I miss you still my special friend,
Sweet memories I hold,
And when I hear that song I see
Those meadows where we strolled.

Dear Francesca

Based on Robert's letter in *The Bridges of Madison County* by Robert James Waller

Just a short time ago – it seems a lifetime –
I was content, self-contained,
A loner, as I told you,
Though not a monk,
A free spirit, carefree,
Needing nobody.

I remember every moment.
Your shy smile when we met,
That magnetism between us,
Your voice, your touch,
The scent of your skin as we embraced,
What happened to me in your arms?

Everywhere I look, I see you,
Every moment, I think of you,
I long to hear your voice,
Caress your cheek
And taste your eager lips.

If ever you can be with me again,
Please call – I'll be there – waiting.

Finding My New Home

I waited in my cage with hopeful heart
(They say that every dog will have his day)
To find a home in which to play a part.

The name I got was written on a chart,
For I was found and brought in as a stray.
I waited in my cage with hopeful heart.

As I was young and wanted a new start,
My loving nature I put on display
To find a home in which to play a part.

My looks were good, my intellect was smart,
Please let someone come without delay.
I waited in my cage with hopeful heart.

A lady saw me – could I win her heart?
I walked with her and showed I would obey,
To find a home in which to play a part.

The next day I was ready to depart,
For she returned to carry me away,
I waited in my cage with hopeful heart
And found a home in which to play a part.

A Basket of Apricots

What was it that drew me to you?
A picture was on my computer –
Not a flattering photograph –
And a naff name,
But I heard a voice:
Go and have a look.

Such a quiet, gentle boy,
The colour of apricots and cream,
Just the right size,
Caged with an oversexed mongrel
That you tolerated, showing
A docile disposition.

I'm not sure, I'll come back tomorrow.
But you had already seeped
Into my soul.
I chose your name as I drove home,
Thought about you all evening,
Dreamed of my new companion.

Next day I took you walking,
Sensed a loving nature,
Desire to please.
This is the dog for you,
That voice in my ear again –
I took you with me.

How right I was to heed that voice.
You slotted into my life
As if you were meant to be there,
Content to have found a home.
You fill my days with sweetness –
My basket of apricots.

Surfeit

Excessive devotion –
The sort that says,
I would give you my last crust –
Might seem like a gift.

But it hints at martyrdom,
Expects appreciation.

The recipient
May sense shackles.
Such sacrifice
Can sow resentment.

Thief

A dismal disorder
Has stolen your memory,
Emptied your brain cells
By some kind of sorcery.

We'd chatter and laugh
About all kinds of topics
From travel, romances,
To old times and ethics.

But now you've succumbed to
Encroaching dependence.
You repeat the same stories,
Eroding my patience.

I'm closing the shutters
At a time when you need me.
A chill has come over
Our bright repartee.

This affliction results in
Shared history lost.
And lays on our friendship
An untimely frost.

The Dream in My Pocket

Tucked into my back pocket for forty years,
I kept a dream –
To live in the great southern land
That was my childhood fascination.

I knew that one day I would go.
What took me so long?

Career demands deflected me,
Love affairs intervened,
The 'points system' put up barriers,
My senior dog needed me,
But I scanned the migrant press,
Never letting the dream wither.

Fortune was kind in my retirement,
A pathway led to a visa.
Emigrating to Australia, at your age! someone snorted,
(I was only fifty-seven)
The house is sold and I leave next week, I retorted.

The day I went to Australia House
To get that precious label in my passport,
I could have danced down the street.
The dream, no longer in my pocket,
Was in my hand.

Just Dreaming

My thoughts go to rural England,
The freedom of rights of way
In the countryside and woodland
And strolls along the canal.

But never to hear the currawong's cry,
Or the magpie's melodious song.

When I feel very cold in the winter,
I long for my cosy home,
With comfortable central heating
And a place to dry my damp clothes.

But never to hear the currawong's cry,
Or the butcherbird's lyrical call.

I remember the radio programmes,
Dramas and afternoon plays,
Quizzes and documentaries,
A book reading just before bed.

But I'd miss the kookaburra's cackle
And the magpie's melodious song.

I think about long summer evenings,
When I sat in the garden till ten,
Never troubled by pesky mosquitoes
Just sipping my wine with content.

But never to hear the currawong's cry,
Or the butcherbird's lyrical call.
I would miss the kookaburra's cackle
And the magpie's melodious song.

The Lighter Side

Poetic Potions

Have you considered, you poets,
That we are a fortunate tribe?
No need to contain our emotions,
Poems are ours to prescribe.

Places that leave an impression,
We treasure these memories in verse.
If we are blue, this can cheer us,
Nostalgia's a qualified nurse.

When love takes a hold of our being
And we feel it's beyond our control,
A sonnet is just the right treatment -
Stanzas expressing the soul.

At a time of great celebration
What better to write than an ode
To record the revels and fanfare
And remember a grand episode.

When we grieve for a pet or a person,
An obituary poem, no less,
Remains as a touching memorial
And helps to relieve our distress.

Don't forget the elixir of humour,
They say it's a tonic to laugh,
So compose those limericks and ditties
And give them your autograph.

Gleaming

My favourite friend's in the bathroom,
It stands there just waiting for me,
Three times a day after eating,
I brush all my choppers with glee.

Those molars, incisors and canines
Are cleaned front and back and beneath,
It freshens my mouth and my outlook,
I really like brushing my teeth.

My dentist thinks I'm a marvel
To have such a mouthful as mine,
For me it's hardly a virtue,
When cleaning my teeth I feel fine.

Every month I buy a new toothbrush,
Maybe blue or magenta or green,
I brush and I floss with abandon,
To keep my pearly whites clean.

The Teddy Bear's Downfall

If you go down to the studio,
Prepare for a big surprise,
If you go down to the studio,
You'd better not idolise,
This teddy bear is not what he seems,
He'll touch you up and shatter your dreams,
Today's the day the teddy bear has his downfall.

If you go down to the studio
To see this teddy bear's art,
If you go down to the studio,
You'd better be pretty smart,
Although he went and painted the Queen,
To you he might do something obscene,
Today's the day the teddy bear has his downfall.

If you go down to the jail today,
You'll see a broken bear,
If you go down to the jail today,
He may be in despair.
Reputation rended to shreds,
Talent no longer turning heads,
Today's the day this teddy bear has his downfall.

A Girl's Best Friend

You may be too old for a miniskirt,
Or midriff-baring shirt,
Too staid for a pop concert,
But you're never too old for gold.

You may be too old to dance till three
At a rave or all-night spree,
Too tired to enjoy the love called free,
But you're never too old for gold.

You may be too old to cut a dash,
Or behave in a manner that's rash,
Youth is an asset gone in a flash,
But you're never too old for gold.

Paradise Found

To Aitutaki I was bound,
With hope that I'd become unwound.
My bungalow was picture-perfect,
Just like the magazines project,
But my Eden had a snake,
It really was a big headache,
Every time I sat outside,
Despite the use of pesticide,
Mosquitoes zoomed right in on me
And very soon I had to flee.

Two days later I departed –
Never one to be downhearted –
To another island place,
Where I had veranda space.
No mosquitoes bothered me,
The gods above had heard my plea.
So I lingered there for longer
On the isle of Rarotonga.

Aitutaki and Rarotonga are in the Cook Islands.

My Fate

When you get older,
You will feel colder,
A workmate said to me.
Your blood will get thinner,
Your body much skinnier,
Was her severe decree.

So what can I do
To avoid this fate?
I won't feel blue,
I'll find a young date.
We'll fly away to a tropical isle,
Laugh in the sun and live in style.

Limericks

The profligate species of man
Reproduced till the Earth overran.
He wasted resources,
Defied Nature's forces,
Then tried to stop what he began.

The inventor is locked in his shed,
Making prototype plans in his head,
While his lady can't wait
To open the gate,
And take her young lover to bed.

Every sport for me is a bore,
Behaviour of fans I deplore,
I cannot perceive
The thrills they receive
When a player alters the score.

Oven Gloves

I tried to make some olive bread,
A simple loaf – the damper sort,
An easy recipe had said
That I could make some olive bread.

It seems that I had been misled
And used more sugar than I ought,
I tried to make some olive bread,
But baked a scone – the damper sort.

Trollittering

There should be a word for the urban scourge
Of trolleys left in the street.
They look so unsightly – does nobody care
About keeping our roads looking neat?

It seems every week I must call to report
Yet another is parked on the verge.
In the past year the problem's got worse
We certainly do need a purge.

There are bins for the litter and most of us try
To do the right thing with our waste,
We do not contaminate rivers and seas,
Viewing debris and trash with distaste.

We are so lucky to live in this place,
With our parks, our rivers and trees,
Trolley pollution needs a solution,
The dumping of trolleys should cease.

Metromania

Attack of metromania,
Whatever can it mean?
A trip to the metropolis
To vary my routine?

Or should I go to Paris
To travel on the train
And watch the city traffic
Beside the River Seine.

Perhaps the Moscow metro
Would be the place to go,
With clean and sparkling stations
Like palaces below.

This pressing metromania,
Before it gets much worse,
I must indulge my passion –
A mania for verse.

www.ingramcontent.com/pod-product-compliance
Lightning Source LLC
Chambersburg PA
CBHW062155100526
44589CB00014B/1849